I0447822

Mandala
Clever Coloring Book

Copyright: Published in the United States by Kenny Tenney
Published December 2016
ISBN-13: 978-1541281066
ISBN-10: 1541281063

Thank you

www.ingramcontent.com/pod-product-compliance
Lightning Source LLC
Chambersburg PA
CBHW051946280526
45789CB00009B/3185
* 9 7 8 1 5 4 1 2 8 1 0 6 6 *